SHATTERED NOT BROKEN BY LIVING VICTORIOUSLY THROUGH THE HOLY SPIRIT

Barbara Brown

All Rights Reserved
Copyright 2015 Barbara Brown
No part of this paper may be reproduced or transmitted, downloaded, distributed, reversed, engineered or stored in or introduced into any information storage and retrieval system in any form or by any means including photocopying and recording whether electronic or mechanical now known or hereinafter invented without permission in writing from the writer.
Published by Barbara Brown   11236@gmail.com

ISBN: 069242153X
ISBN 13: 9780692421536

INTRODUCTION

The Memoirs of Barbara Brown

The ways I took it back when I felt no one understood or cared. It was through the following obstacles good or bad that I was being prepared for, by sharing my story will encourage the reader, who has had the same crisis to be able to overcome and move forward in their lives. I hope you will be able to leave the past behind like water under the bridge. "Sometimes God give you a taste of good and double great!" I am proud of me today, because I can tell you how to get through it because I've been through and was able to overcome.

After moving on forward when you have done all you can, by standing up to the truth. Even if it meant other people would not understand and you had to deal with their pain, but you have to continue to stand for the truth of the meaning of life's disappointments. From the truth they could not see. For those that can see can say "I can see much clearer because God is not finished with me yet, so Get Ready!"

I will share my story from the age of four to my present age of sixty three. This nonfiction will share the bad experiences I faced by not have the right adults in my life to give me parental support during my younger years, which lead my siblings and me to be placed in the foster care system.

I remember living in a one room in a rooming house. The building was located in a poor rundown neighborhood. My mother was a young woman, age eighteen with six children, all girls. We all had different fathers with three last names. Three of my older siblings had the same last name, the middle two had a different name and the youngest had her father's name. Our ages range from six to one year. Later on in life, two of the oldest would follow into my mother's footsteps giving up their children to foster care, turning to drugs and dying at a very early age.

CHAPTER ONE

My Younger Years with My Siblings

As myself and all my siblings lay on the hard covered floor and there were no warm blankets to keep us warm, My mother laid in the bed with our step father with comfortable sheets. And I remember looking at the window with no curtains to cover them. My mother would leave every day to go to work. We were left alone with the mean step father who introduced us to the life of sex. This was done in the absence of my mother who was never around. I always wondered to this day did she know what he was doing. I felt it was very selfish of her to allow her children to be denied a bed to sleep in while the over sexed mean step father was allowed to enjoy the comfortable bed, and then taking advantage by sexually molesting children who were left alone, from not knowing right from wrong and naive, to being forced to have oral sex with an adult male. After this went on for a while my oldest sister decided to tell my mother who acted so surprised. She packed all us up only to move us into a rundown house with no heat and we only had on our underwear. She would leave us alone only to sit on a couch together. The only thing to eat was white sugar in a large jar. This was our daily food to eat. There were stairs but for some reason we were not allowed to go. I never understood why? May be she had a nice comfortable bed for her men.

Being left alone men would come in and give my sister candy to sit on their laps. I always had trusting issues, so for some reason I was not turned on to my stepfather or men who used their tactics to lure children to have sex like it was the right thing to do.

Eventually my grandmother came to take us with her, because my stepfather found out where we lived and took his daughter the youngest sibling. My mother came from who knows where and told us she was going to get our sister. This was a joke because she never came back. We were all placed in separate foster homes. This was a disaster because when you separate sibling they never know anything about each other. They only remember the past and have no future together. My mother never came to visit us or any of our fathers. So to this day, I never met my father. The only name written on my birth certificate is T. H. Brown. We were able to visit my grandmother who stayed in a studio apartment. She worked as a maid for a Caucasian family who were very rich and their house was on a lake. One day my grandmother took me to visit. From this visit I pointed to the lake and said one day I would live by a lake and would never clean anyone's floors. My grandmother suffered with swollen legs and feet from always being on her feet. She would let us sleep in the one bed with her. The room smelled like ???. She loved to cook soul food and listen to Mahalia Jackson gospel music. I wish my grandmother would have taken us to rise. This way we could have been together. Maybe she wanted to, but she never came to visit us for the few years. We were in foster care. It seems like my mother disappeared. I only saw her years later when she came out of jail.

Why are children allowed to be molested by relatives and strangers? This is like a secret that is kept in silence and shame. Time is changing, allowing everyone to share their secrets. So others will not hide in darkness by allowing their feeling to enter in their future relationships. Some people that have been molested put up a wall to hide their feelings. There are those who don't care they let it all hang out by becoming pernicious to gain power and control to get back what was taken. Then there is the other group who are neutral pretending it never happened. They overcome by dressing themselves up in sheep's clothing lying "saying that did not happen to me." Even the parents of the children do the same saying you are lying stop lying. You should not tell lies. No matter what group you fall in, tell someone. Let someone know. You are not alone. This will help young women and men not to be afraid to share their story, by not feeling ashamed. This will also encourage them to let go and move on by overcoming.

CHAPTER TWO

Going into the Foster Care System

After leaving the stable environment of living with my grandmother the Department of Social Service came to place siblings and me in separate foster homes. This would be the last few years I would see three of my siblings. My mother never returned after this time. My oldest sister, me, next and the younger one were placed in a temporary foster home. The foster mother had a nice home, but was very religious. We all shared the same bedroom in a small country town located in New Jersey. We were given all the basic necessity of food & shelter. It seemed like the majority of our time was spent on being in church day and night. We did not attend school, are around people to spend time with. This time in my life I had the feeling that something was missing, but I was too young to know. The foster mom could be mean at times if anyone of us rejected to the time we spent in church. It really did not matter if we were hungry or needed to go to the bathroom. It was more important to put church service first instead of our personal needs. Sometimes we would have to urinate on ourselves. Then we would be beaten for not waiting till service ended.

I thought this was very unfair, because we were too young and had not been exposed to the life of church. At this time I did not understand why we had to spend so much time in church which to me was not important. For some reason before I could look around we were taken away and placed with another foster home.

My new foster mother Mrs. Flin and father Mr. Flin lived in a nice house with a large back yard in New Jersey. There was a big back yard with a large garden with vegetables growing. There was an apple and peach tree. My foster mom would preserve the peaches and apples for the winter. She also taught us how to make grape jelly and wine from the grapes. The fruits would be stored in glass jars located in the closet of the basement of the house. During the holiday she would bring out the wine and fruit preserve during the winter. My foster mother never bought vegetables or fruits from local store. My foster dad whom I looked up to like a father I never had. He never disrespected us or his wife. He adored her and would pull the chair out for her to sit down. They never argued in front of us or raised their voice. My foster mom would just send us to bed if we disobeyed. We only received a spanking if we did something really bad. The only thing I regret is I never understood why we could not socialize with our peers. One day when I came home, my foster was not there. I decided to wait for her at the neighbor's house. When my foster mom came home we all were beaten with a switch off the tree. To this day I do not like to visit people in their homes. I become very uncomfortable when I do visit. Maybe my foster mom was being over protective because she did not want anything to happen to us. Because of course we were called the foster children. This was very well known because of living in a small town in Asbury Park, New Jersey. Everyone liked to gossip and mind everyone's business. At this time I couldn't really understand. Now that I'm older you cannot always trust everyone. I expected this and would not go to the neighbor's house when my foster mom was not home.

Life became very secure for me living there. It was like I had finally had a secure family life. My oldest sister and I shared the same bedroom and my younger sister was able to have her own room. At time she would urinate on herself, so maybe it was better she slept alone. Eventually my foster mother adopted a boy who was up for adoption as she had always wanted a son. Then later she expected an older foster female who did listen. She would sneak next door with the boy who lived there. They eventually got married and had five children. She was not interested in education. My foster mother would not allow us to speak to her, but it was exciting to hear about the boy next door. She also spoke Spanish and would teach us some words. Outside of that we had a good life. I loved school and was a student. I loved to sit and read the newspaper to my foster mom. She would listen to me read as she washed the dishes. I was reading very well by age five. During the summer we would walk in the summer heat to the library. The only place we went was to church every Sunday, the movies and library during summer break. I loved going in the large basement dressing up in her old clothes. The basement was very cool in the summer. If we went outside we would take an umbrella to keep the sun away. I also enjoyed riding my bicycle, jumping rope and playing with my boxer dog Primo. He really loved children and would allow us to ride on his back like a horse. We always got dressed up for Easter and Christmas. One of our neighbors would give us her daughter's dress they outgrew. I loved those wide skirts on the dress. I would wear a wide slip with my patch leather shoes. To this day I always keep the patch leather shoes and my rain coat. I never gave my foster mom any reason to punish me, because I enjoyed learning and she enjoyed teaching me. The school was very supportive of us and did not make us feel isolated. My foster mom encouraged me to love dolls and do their hair. When I got older I bought a doll collection from all over the world. I still love to corn roll my hair in different hair styles. I am happy to say my foster mom and dad gave me stability during my younger years. Later on in my life it was what I needed to sustain me during rough times. Even when I became older I kept contact with my foster mom and dad until they both passed away. They remained in the same church for fifty years and were still married till their death. This is very rare in today's generation. People do not stay married very long. It's like a revolving door. They can walk away at the drop of a hat. Marriage has become a convenience, not a long time commitment. During the past there were more family time and less outside influence. We spent every evening at the dinner table. This way we all share how our day went. We would laugh when someone past gas or belched. Everyone would act like who did this and we would play a game not me and blame the dog who was under the table waiting for food to fall. After dinner we would take turns washing the dishes and getting prepared for school. We were only allowed to watch the daily news and one show on television. It was very important for us to say our grace before dinner and our prayers at bed time.

One thing I never understood why we had to attend funerals of people we did not know. I remember a young woman wearing a beautiful balloon dress. She had died at a very young age. I guess I was too young to understand why a beautiful young woman could die so young. Now that I'm older death has no age from 0 – 100 it doesn't matter when your time come for whatever reason we don't know when. Even when it's not your time death can come from another person or accident. This is why we have to live life to the fullest and enjoy each moment. You cannot allow anyone to predict your future if they do not have your interest. We have to be careful who we bring into our lives. The wrong people may cause you to stumble and fall. Even lose your life over nonsense. This is maybe why my foster mom was protective of us. When we are young we cannot always see into the future till we get there.

Older people like to say take your time and smell the roses. After a few years passed – my foster mother shared with me she was getting older and would not be able to raise us. The only one she kept was my foster brother. I felt very angry about a new separation. I became very depressed about what laid ahead. I began to fail in school. I even punched myself in the nose to make it bleed. I became outraged not understanding why? Everything was going so well why did I have to leave? I was a good girl and never gave my foster mother any problem. I was always very obedient by listening to her and my foster dad. If I had been able to stay I knew I would become successful by even becoming a veterinarian doctor. I really loved animals and would have studied very hard. I continued to act out in school and was sent to see the counselor. He asked why I was falling from an A to D student. I told him my two sisters and me would be going to a new foster home. He tried to encourage me, but inside my mind I really did not care.

I began to play hooky hanging in the street. This fascinated me to see men and women hanging in the bars. One day I saw my foster dad drinking in the bar. This really surprised me to know this. He never drinks at home. Sometime he would drink out a bottle and tell us it was his cough medicine. He would make us laugh by coughing. It was like my foster parents did not want to expose us to bad habit such as drinking, eating sweets, and sexual behavior. One day I came home early and found my foster mother having sex in the kitchen with the neighbor's husband. This really shocked me to this day. It is like a picture in my mind. She made me feel guilty by blaming me for walking in, she stated "don't you dare do that again". I always felt upset about this–Even though people attend church and appear to be perfect they are not. People are not always what they seem. I was learning this very early in life to prepare me for the future.

Besides that I still loved my foster mom whom I called momma Flin and my foster dad daddy Larry. After I left a few years they sold the house and the dog Primo died. My foster brother went in to the army. They both were older and daddy Larry had cancer.

They made me laugh of when I was living with them. We had taken a ride in the country like we would always pack up to take short trips to Pennsylvania and New York. During one of our trips I would eat all the blueberries off the trees. One day I got the worst stomach and we all laughed. I would lie next to them on the bed remembering the early days how my time flies. I stayed in touch with them both till they both died. They were able to see me become a teacher and have my own family. I still miss them today but I know when my life is over they will be waiting for me in the sunset.

I wrote three poems for the love they both showed me when I did not have my own parents there for me. The love they showed, gave me a lot of strength during trials I faced. But I always tried my best to stay on the right path because of their guidance. Here are the three poems I dedicated to momma Flin and daddy Larry Flin.

Love from Those Who Were There
When Our Parents Were Not

You took the place of our real parents for reasons we
don't understand
I'm sure they meant well, but could not be there
when we needed them
I must forgive them and not grudge their absence,
But know there were was someone who could
take their place
Because they knew we still needed to be
loved no matter what,
So they decided to share their love with
someone like me.

Dedicated to my foster mother Mrs. Luscill Flin and my foster father Mr. Larry Flin. Thank you for helping me become the person I am through the love you gave me.

Love & Peace,
Barbara Brown

From a Mother's love
This experience will be the comfort of your life.
Your mother's love will never die
Even when you have moved on.
This memory will always be there.
The comfort from her eyes to let you know the
Strength she has given you
Will be the best love she has offered you forever

Dedicated to my foster mom and those entire mothers, who raised their children to become successful citizens.

From the love of a Father
His strength is the most you could imagine
The love you shared will have no end.
You will always remember his love.
That will bring you in to the height of existence
You will look for his love in all your relationships
But no one can compare to the love of your father.

Dedicated to my foster father and to all those fathers who gave love allowing their children to become responsible role models.

CHAPTER THREE

New Foster Home Experience

My new foster parents owned a big house in the country of New Jersey. They had acres of land with animals. My sisters and I had our own bedroom. We had lots of home cooked meals. They really adored me, because I was tall with a Barbie doll figure. I loved my own bedroom. They treated me like a princess. They bought me all the latest clothes to make me look nice. Of course we attended church, because her husband was the pastor. The church was very large with acres of land. When church service ended we would eat fried fish and chicken. I was able to put hot sauce on my food, to this day I love spicy food. Everyone adored me and made over me. I was made to feel very welcomed, but I really didn't care. I really missed mamma Flin and daddy Larry whom I was taken from. No matter what they did made a difference. I already made up my mind I just didn't care. I was given an allowance to spend as I pleased. I saved up the money because I planned on leaving. I was sick of the foster care system changing me from place to place. There was never a caseworker to see how we were doing. It was as though we always had to deal with our own emotion sink or swim. Well I decided to find a way to swim as far as I could. I felt I could move away on my own and everything would be alright.

We started a new school my sisters and I. The school bus would pick us up, because the school was too far away for us to walk. When I arrived at school I did not want to be in class. There was nothing to keep me interested. I started to smoke cigarettes and curse. My new foster mom got hold of the news and asked me why? I don't remember what I said all I know was I did give a hoot any more nothing matter. She did everything she could to make me happy taking me shopping, but it was like I gave up. After I saved a few dollars I told my sisters I was leaving and would come back to get them. Who was I fooling I was only thirteen and couldn't take care of myself. They gave me their allowance so I would have enough money to leave. I felt really bad to leave them wishing to this day I could have taken them with me. I guess we all would have to live in the town of Asbury Park on the streets. I thought I was leaving them in good hands but they eventually ran away too. It seems the foster father who was a pastor was molesting some of the foster children.

I heard about this after I left. There was nothing I could say or do. I wish to this day he would be punished for his actions. You know to this day I don't even remember their names. I still remember momma Flin and daddy Flin but not them.

One day while I was attending school I had bought all my allowance to run away. Before school ended I walked to the bus stop and came back to the town of Asbury Park, New Jersey. I went wild and I mean wild. I started drinking gypsy rose wine and put tattoos on my arm. I would hang out at people house drinking and smoking.

Then I met an older guy named Donnie he was tall, dark and handsome. He was in college and on the football team. This was my first love. I could get enough of him now I was free to have all the sex I wanted, till I become pregnant. He was called to go to Vietnam War, so again I was left on my own to figure out what to do. I really loved him with all my heart I wrote his name on my right arm with a broken heart. A few of us would meet up at different people house to drink wine. One of the guys took a needle with Indian ink and gave us tattoos. we were lucky we never got an infection.

I even would ride around in convertible cars with the hood down with some of the local girls. We would put blond color in our hair so the sun would make it bright. I was just so wild. One day while I was pregnant I went to one of the hang out spots. I was there with a few boys and the only female. They decided to have a contest of who could drink the most wine. Well I didn't know any better and felt I had to show them. Well I really showed them, by getting ??? drunk what did I know and being pregnant. I went into the bedroom to lie down and one of the boy raped me, but I was so drunk it didn't matter. I never told anyone or talked about for years. This became my second secret. One day I was walking home and the same thing happened. It was like I became numb to anything that happened. I didn't have a place to live, so I was left with no choice, but to be a homeless teenager with no family or a place to live. I decided to ask around since I was pregnant, so I thought I should have an abortion. A young man told me he knew someone and we set up a date to meet. When the date came his people never showed up, so he told me to insert a hanger in my vagina to abort my child. I tried this, but I became scared when I saw some blood. He later told me to take a bottle of quinine pills they only made my ears ring. I decided I would just buy a girdle and walk around holding my stomach in. People would ask me if I was pregnant I lied and said no. I would walk on the back streets to avoid people.

My boyfriend had gone to the army so we had no contact. This was during the sixties. I use to love that song "Bring the boys home". I wish he could have been there. We both love the songs from this time upon the roof and a lot of the Drifter's songs. Years later we ran into each other, but he had contacted a disease from the army and became very sick. He asked me "What happened to the baby? I told him I had eventually given him up for adoption. He told me his sister could have helped me out, but it was too late. Eventually he later passed away from the disease and he never met his son. I left the small town of Asbury Park and moved to Bronx, New York where my grandmother came and took me to.

CHAPTER FOUR

Living in the Bronx, NY

Coming to New York in the Bronx 1765 Walton Ave. In order to get there you had to take the subway train. The subway speeds down the rails about 100 miles a minute. You can see poles on the side and a walk way path. Each train stop has the numbers, so you will know when you reach your destination. My grandmother lived at the 175th street exit is where we got off. We had to walk down from the Grand Concourse. The Grand Concourse was where a lot of doctors and lawyers lived. Their pent apartment could have up to thirteen rooms. In the middle of the street was set up like a park with rows of grass and trees. There were benches for the rich to sit on. The black nannies who took care of the babies of the rich would sit to give them sunshine as they lay in their strollers. Buses would come up and down the street letting lots of people on and off. This was the way New Yorkers traveled back and forth. Very few people would drive their cars. There were rows of tall buildings close together. It was like there was very little space in between. This was a big change for me coming from a small town in New Jersey where people owned their home and there was plenty of space for children to run around. The buildings did not have backyards, so children would play on the sidewalk. There were grocery stores on every corner. The stores were mostly owned by the Spanish people. My grandmother's building went up to the sixth floor, but she lived on the first floor. There was an elevator to go to the higher floors. Each floor had at least eight apartments. It was like people lived on top of each other like rats what I say no room to move around.

My grandmother worked for a rich family upon the concourse. The husband was a very rich doctor named Dr. Klein. She was their maid to take care of their household chores. My grandmother never completed high school or went to college. Later on in her life she retired with a small social security check. She never drove a car or wanted to own any property. She suffered from high blood pressure but would never take medication. She loved to drink gin every Thursday when she got paid. She would cook a lot of pork. Most of her food had some kind of fat and was used to fry chicken and make biscuits. She would always put fat back in her collard greens and cabbage. My grandmother lived in a small one bed room. There was a small kitchen, living room foyer, and bathroom. She enjoyed cooking for her friends who would visit from New Jersey. They would just sit around and talk about the good old days. Now we were living in the late 1967. Things were different for them now that they are older. Having a baby was very rarely heard of. Family members would raise the children born out of wed lock, so the young women could start a new life. This would allow her to marry a man with no children. My grandmother tried to set me up with one of her friend's son who had been in the army, but I didn't want to marry someone because I was pregnant.

Now being fourteen and pregnant was not easy. I could not go out like other young women. They would invite me to the movies and my grandmother would say you can't go out you have a baby to think about, your fun days are over. This made me feel trapped. She always made me do a lot of chores around the house. After my son Darry Brown was born, I had turned fifteen in July my son was also born in July 2, 1967 in Manhattan at the French Hospital. I spent all my time taking care of him back and forth to the hospital. This was very depressing for me not being able to attend school or hang out with my peers.

I began to resent have a baby and my grandmother became very mean to me like she didn't care how I felt. She would just come from work and eat her soul food and drink her gin.

I never understood why she liked the taste because it tastes nasty to me.

Eventually while my grandmother was at work I called the social services to take my baby. This was very hard for me it still hurts to this day. He was adopted by a family in Queens, NY. They owned a nice big house and could not have any children. They had a bedroom set up for him. He was very cute and playful look just like me. I hope before I leave this life I would like to see him. My grandmother said before she died he is going to find you "I hope, so I would love to know I made the right decision. I could not give him the life his adoptive parents could. I was just too young".

Shattered Not Broken by Living Victoriously Through the Holy Spirit

Dear Darry Brown

*I hope you had a good life
I want you to know I will always love you.
I know your name was changed
I pray someone will tell you the truth.
I hope you forgive me for giving you away.
I was left with no choice by not having any money
I wanted you to have a better life
I pray you did and your adopted parents were good to you.
I look for your face everywhere I go hoping to find you.
I called everyone for help, but there was nothing they could do.
I just trust in God that one day I will see your face in my face.*

Love mom,
Barbara Brown

CHAPTER FIVE

Living on the Streets of Bronx, NY

For a while it was like freedom from all the adults in my life. I could feel free to make my own decisions. I would just live on the streets day and night. A group of young people who ran away from their homes would hang together. We came from a different race, and economic background. At times I would visit my grandmother to get some food to eat. One day my mother came from jail and asked me to live with her. She told me "Just because I had a baby I wasn't grown." Now who was she to tell me what to do since she was no where around when we were placed in foster care and how she has the nerve to give advice. My grandmother's apartment became the place for all my sister to come to during hard times. My mother even stayed. I guess this was my grandmother's way of making up for us being placed in foster care. She would make holiday dinner so anyone could come. After some of my siblings came from the different foster home staying anywhere they could. They could always stay at grandma's to eat or drink. She would just talk about each other like we were dogs. We would just steal her food and take it to where we could sleep.

You had to be really down and out when you came to her. It wasn't like there was any love to get or good advice it was a always criticism. She hated my mother and my mother hated her. They never seemed to forgive each other for their past. They spent their life fighting and grudging each other. I use to feel sorry for my mother the way my grandmother treated her. At times you could see how this really hurt her, but my grandmother could never forgive her for the accident she caused on the loss of her baby. My grandmother reminds her everytime she came around by keeping a picture of the baby in the casket. My mother was supposed to give her first born to make up for this accident. My mother did not keep her bargain, so my grandmother never forgave her. Later on when my grandmother died my mother had her ashes placed with my oldest sister in the cemetery. I guess this was my mother's way of making up at the end.

Well I just wanted to be free of all the drama. I really couldn't change how they lived their lives, but I was going to try to become a forgiving person and not carry grudges to my grave. I just lived most of the time on the streets of Davidson Ave. This was during the late sixties where there was a big flow of the drug dope. The majority of the young people began to shot it up their nose. They would just walk around like Zombies nodding their head up and down. I was afraid to try it, because I witness some of them taking a over dose. There were a lot of rooming house to hang around. We could go there to wash out our clothes and use the bathroom. Some of the young people began to shoot up with the needle in the bathroom. They were put in the tub and given a shot of salt with water which revived them. When they came to they didn't remember what happen only to shoot drugs again. Now if people from the hood did not like you they would not bring you out. Some people would be thrown off the roof. People who worked would be robbed and left to die with their pockets hanging out. It was a doggie world. If you were from the hood everyone looked out for you if not you put your life in other's hand. They all looked out for me giving me money they made shooting dice. I would eat free pizza and drink the red and purple drink filled with a lot of sugar. Some of the older guys would set me up with an account at the store to get what I needed. When they got their monthly check they would pay the bill. Sometime the drug dealers did like me hanging around since I didn't want to try drugs, so they would threaten my life, but there was always someone around to take their life. A man threatened to get me to do drugs if it was the last thing he did, well two days later he has found shot in the head. My oldest sister started to come around and began to us dope. I begged her not to but she would not listen. She started to drink a lot and became a lesbian. I tried to look out for her, but I guess the foster care system and my mother failed her never giving her the love she needed. She had children that she didn't raise following my mother's footsteps. My grandmother wind up raising her daughter Jahell, who later was adopted when she was passed away. My sister Majorie found an older man who would give her all the liquor and drugs she needed. She was in a very abusive relationship. She never went to school or owned anything of her own. She just lived day to day until she died at age twenty eight. This really hurt me because she was my oldest sister, but she never found any happiness on this earth. She died in a comma in the hospital the doctor said she had just given up. I wish I could have done more but I was one year younger than her living in the hood with no job or money. Years later I put a tombstone down for her and my middle sister Sarah who living the same life style and died at age thirty eight. They both deserved a better life on this earth but I hope where they are at they are given the love and peace they never received so. One day I will join them to have the sisters I wasn't able to have on earth, but later in heaven. The tombstone stated "Loved But Never Forgotten". So I dedicated this poem to them.

From the Love of a Sister
The love of a sister can be very challenging
But they should be someone you can depend
You will share the most intimate moments as you go along
But there should always be forgiveness through each gentle storm
The time you've spent as you both grow p
To know you had each other to lean on
During your secrets you both shared.

Dedicated to my sisters beloved Majorie RIP, Sarah RIP, and Betty unknown and to all those sisters who showed each other love, by letting each other know you could depend on them.

Peace & Love,
Barbara Brown

CHAPTER SIX

Spending Time with My Mother

Well I did spend some time with my mother. She tried, but I guess it was too late. I went back to Taft High School to try and finish. I was feeling what it was like to be a teenager. My mother would give me money to shop at Alexander's. I really loved shopping for clothes. I would wake up early to dress up for school. Now the boys were really attracted to my Barbie doll shape. They would throw pencils at my butt when I walked up the stairs. I always wind up with the cutest boy. One day he came to my apartment where my mother lived with a group of his friend like a gang. I was really impressed, because all the girls at school wanted to date him, so they hated my guts. Well I never got along much with females even when I got older. They always felt the males gave me more attention than them. Then I really didn't care I felt like you will like me or hate me for your own reasons not mine. You can hate me for who I am or where I came from it doesn't matter why or the reason why one color in the front and another in the back. Why can't we become one?.

I began to enjoy school, because my foster mom encouraged me to work hard and supported me I always loved to study and read. My mother met a new boyfriend who reminds me of a street hustler. She had a seventh child by a good man Sonny who really loved her, but he wasn't good enough. She always needed the bad boys. I really liked Sonny RIP. He was really good for her. He stayed in touch with me when I started my own family. He would come and give me money any time I needed it. My mother became angry later on because she only used him. Eventually in her older age she wind up with two more children that eventually was taken away name Deon Leon and Marie. They were all adopted in her older years. She continued to repeat the same pattern. I had given up one child for adoption and was not going to end up like my mother with nine children. I did everything I could not to become pregnant. I did not want to live with my mother anymore with her man and three more children a total of nine. Then I decided to leave school and go back to the streets. I ran from place to place just out of control. I finally got my first job and was finally making some new strives. I got my first room in one of the rooming house. I was finally being responsible by paying rent. I met a young lady on the job we work as a file clerk in Manhattan. She had given up her son like me for adoption. We both share our story and became good friends at work. Every day at lunch time we would go to Woolworth's store to eat chicken. I really enjoyed her company. I had lied how old I was to the supervisor of the office, because I didn't have a birth certificate. She was from another race and she filed for me to get my birth certificate. I always thought I was born on one date and found it was another. I really enjoyed my first job. I even went back to Taft High School to get my transcript. I was told you didn't get pregnant yet. I guess she knew what she was talking about because not too far later I did become pregnant with my son Calvin Brown at age 16 and then Stanly Brown RIP at age eighteen. By nineteen, I had three children I eventually tied my tubes in my early twenties not to have any more children.

The Supervisor retired and the new supervisor was not very nice. She put me in the storage department transporting large boxes. This was not the job I wanted to do. I enjoy having my own desk and learning how to file paper as a clerical worker. During this time the landlords where I lived sold the rooming building. The new landlord did not have record of the rent I paid, because I paid with cash. So I was put out in the street, since I had no receipts to prove I had paid the rent. I learned from this experience and to this day I never throw out any of my papers. I still have my first telephone bill when Verizon was Bell Atlantic. It's good to keep your hard copies in case the computer system shut down. Years later I had paid a bill to the city then they sent me a bill but I had saved all my old bills. They stated "If I didn't have them I would have to pay again".

Here I go again back in the street with nowhere to live. I met my new boyfriend and fell in love. We would make passionate love every chance we got. He lived with a roommate and had a job. He also had his own room. Well you know what come next with this entire hot and heavy sex yes you know pregnant again.

I would spend some nights with him but some of the older people took a liking to me and would let me babysit for their children to earn money. This made it easy for me not to hang in the street being pregnant. One day I went back and wind up getting into a fight with a girl who mistakes me for the wrong person putting her sister in the hospital. We fought like cats and dogs in the gutter. She even bit on my breast and leg. I must have forgotten. I was pregnant and we stopped fighting. I didn't even have money to go to the doctor, so I had to get medicine from a friend. She told me I needed to get away from those streets. I knew I had to make a change.

CHAPTER SEVEN

Becoming Responsible as a Pregnant Young Woman

I began to turn to older people for good solid advice. There was an older man named Danny and his wife Marie. He had retired and was a supervisor in a building away from where I would hang out. I enjoyed my visit with them. They would give me clothes people had thrown away. I was also given food to eat. I loved those large hamburgers he would make they taste so good. He would share stories of Montego Bay, it seems he really missed. There he would babysit his grandchildren when they come from school. His wife worked as a nurse and he was waiting for her to retire. He had bought a nice home for them to move. He always warned me to be careful of some people. They can really hurt you. He would tell me stories of beautiful young women who lost their life. He told me never to leave my drink unattended. People can put something in it to hurt you. He taught me what foods were healthy to eat. Danny always told me one day you will do something great. I told him look at me I am pregnant and don't have a GED. He would always say "I might not be around but you will do great things". It was like he was predicting my future. He would always say "when I pass away I am going to leave you in my will". I continued to visit them most of the time until I had my son Calvin. He would continue to give me food and clothes. One day during one of my visit he had a stroke and was taken to the hospital. I had moved on in my life. Years later I found out he and his wife had moved into their home, because she had retired. I went to visit to see him. He was left alone with very little food to eat. He shared "His wife Marie had passed away". I bought him soap a few times till his daughter had the neighbor to tell me not to come back. I did not want any trouble, so I did. I will always thank him for the time we spent together. In a way he was like a grandparent I needed in my life RIP till we meet again. I did go on to receive my GED, Three masters and a five year degree in Theology, I also was acknowledged in the Daily Newspaper and received two community awards for the work I did with children. This is my fifth book I am writing Praise to God, Thank You for All You Done and where you brought me from.

I want to share this poem to show how Danny showed me the love of a grandparent.

There is no greater love
Their memories will be treasured forever.
The way they spoil us when our parent said no
The way they were always there when our parents were not
No matter what we could always depend
On the love they gave us when no one was there
Thank you grandparents for all your precious love.

Dedicate to my friend Danny and to all those grandparents who had to raise their grandchildren, by starting all over after raising their own. Hats off to you for doing a great job.

Peace & Love,
Barbara Brown

Life was still challenging one of the ladies I babysit for helped me get on public assistant. She wanted me to stay with her, but they told me, I could get my own place and would pay the rent. She had her own children and a husband and I was pregnant and really wanted my own family. I really appreciate all she did for me giving me a place to stay and the best food in the world, she cooked every day. When you walked in her home it was always clean and the windows were steaming with that smell of home cooked food. A friend of hers made me some maternity clothes because I was getting bigger.

I found a one room place in a rooming house. My son's father would give me money time to time. He would buy me a bucket of fried chicken. I would eat it for breakfast, lunch, and dinner with lots of hot sauce. Some diet for being pregnant. I spent most of my time listening to people run up and down the stairs. We all share the bathroom and kitchen. One of the tenants who were over three hundred pounds loved to cook home fries everyday with onions. I would eat a few, but that seem like the only thing he could afford like me with just chicken. There was a young lady who loved to dress up and meet her boy friend who came from the army. She did not have any children just cute as a button. Her name was Cookie I wonder if she's still living. I admired watching her get dressed, listening to her stories about her boyfriend. It was so exciting since I was pregnant. I would listen for her to come home at night, because she always ran very fast up the stairs. I was always glad she came home safely.

One day I lifted the television and my water broke. I began to leak and did not know what to do. I did not have any money to take the bus or a cab. I decided to put a towel between my legs and walk two miles to the hospital. This was really scary for me not having anyone to turn to. When I arrived at the hospital they turned me away because I was not in labor. I was seven months pregnant. I told them I did not have money to return home. They gave me money for transportation. When I return home my neighbor told me to go back and my son was born prematurely. The oxygen did not reach his brain so he had to stay in an incubator for a while. They thought he would not survive. He weighed only two pounds. I spent all my time at the hospital, till he gained his weight. If you could see him how at age 46 and over two hundred pounds, you would never believe he weighed so little. Life can change at any time. Thank God he came through I never understood why the hospital did not kept me. Before he was released the owner of the rooming said "Children were not allowed to live in a rooming house," so I was able to find a studio apartment. It was really nice; I was able to take care of my new baby. Social service signed me up for parenting classes. I even was assigned a visiting nurse who showed me how to care for my premature baby. The first few years he was always sick. I spent a lot of time at the children's clinic. My social worker Dorthy Harris whom I will always cherish was great. She worked with me to give me all the support I needed. She became my role model and I knew I wanted to be a social worker—in the future.

The following poem is dedicated to all the good friends who came in and out my life. I want to thank you for being there through the good and bad times. Even though I did not have a real family you all played a role in my life for the family I didn't have. You were able to feel a lot of those missing voids in my life. I know some of you have moved on or passed on, but I will always remember you, so I share this poem to thank you.

From the Love of a Real Friend
A friend is someone you can depend.
They will never let you down.
They will always be there till the end.
Even through difficult times.
You can depend on a good friend
Through the storms,
Through the tears
They will never let you down.
This is when you know you have a friend
They will never talk about or turn their back on you.
When you are going through a tough time
but will support you till the end.

Dedicated to some of my best friend for over twenty five years Diana, Emma RIP, Mamie, Dorthy Harris and Clare, who have shown me what a good friend is and to all of you who have been blessed to have friends that were there for you.

CHAPTER EIGHT

Living in My First Apartment

My new place was located on 181 in the Bronx. The neighborhood was located away from the bad section. Most of the buildings went up to five floors. There were a few private homes people lived in. A lot of the people had jobs, so there was less hanging around. I met a nice husband and wife, Mr. and Mrs. Morris. I could go visit them, they had six girls and no boys. Her husband always wanted a boy.

My small studio apartment was located on the sidewalk level. The windows faced the sidewalk. It came with furniture, a dinning room set and a studio couch that let out into a bed. I had all the appliances to be comfortable. There was a empty corner, so I bought a crib for my baby. I put up some cute curtains and bought all kinds of decorations. The Department of Social Services gave me money to buy pots and dishes. I would see my sons father time to time. I loved the neighborhood and loved to dress my son up in his cute outfits. I would put him in a stroller to show him off. One day I bought him a white and navy blue outfit. I went to the store and left him with a neighbor. When I returned she had given him a chocolate ice cream bar. He had made such a mess all over his outfit. The neighbor said he is a boy and they should get dirty. He was my first born and I was over protective. I finally had someone I could really love and care for. I made sure he had food and clothes. I wanted to be a great mom.

Then I became pregnant with my third son Stanley Brown. I made sure I took better care of myself. Now that I received public assistance and medicard. I could attend the prenatal clinic. He weighed eight pounds when he was born. Now that I had two children who were one year a part it was more difficult. I bought them a double stroller for twins. I would take them to visit my neighbor. She fell in love with Stanley and loved to watch him. Sometimes I would leave him, but she would not always watch him he would be left dirty running around. Mrs. Morris asked me if she could raise him, because she wanted a son I told her no. I had gave up one son and was never going to give up another. I am glad I didn't, because he only lived for eighteen years.

I would have felt worse if I was not around. Eventually I need a larger place, so I packed up and moved to Jersey City leaving my apartment. I was not able to get welfare and had to work in a factory. I had to find a babysitter. The neighbor was coming back from a lot of building that were abandoned. They were working on them, but did not complete them. There was no heat or electricity. Me and my children slept in the dark. The landlord promised to have heat, but he never did, so I returned back to the Bronx, NY. I was not going to allow my children to suffer with no heat and lights. Even though I had a job and could, pay the rent I decided to leave. A part of me wanted to be able to work and not get welfare. You had to always stay in contact with your case worker who was always in your business. They monitored all the money you spent and did not want the children's fathers hanging around. They would do home visits to make sure of this.

Even though I did not want to return back I had no choice. I called the case worker who "asked me why did I leave"? I told her I wanted to be able to work. She told me to come back and she would give me money for a new apartments so I did. When I return back to the Bronx, the apartment was available, but the landlord refused to give it back to me because I had left without telling him and had took the refrigerator. There was not one at the new place and I needed to keep milk in it for my baby. Even though there was no electricity. I really felt bad about, what I had to do and regreted, what did I done. It did teach me a lesson you never know when you have to go back. It's important to treat people right, because you never know when you will need them again.

    A few blocks away a landlord owned a two family house. He had three bed rooms and lived alone. He told me I could rent two of the bedroom for myself and two boys. It was a nice house very sunny and lots of space. There was plenty of furniture, so I did not have to buy any. The welfare gave me a monthly check to pay rent and buy food. Wow I bought so much food. I really loved my new place. The larger bedroom was in front and I gave it to the boys. There were so many windows all around I only had to go up the one flight of stairs. There was a large backyard for the boys to play. I never understood why the landlord lived alone with all this room. He never bothered anyone he was always a nice gentlemen, sort of funny looking sometime he would take a drink and stay in his room. I was finally happy with so much space-living in a house reminded me of my foster parents home.

CHAPTER NINE

Letting The Devil Move In

An older lady I met named Doris lived in the neighborhood around the corner. She had looked out for me when my son Calvin became sick. She had one son and was involved in an international relationship. Her husband was a drug addict and was put in jail. She lived alone with her son. She was a good mom making sure she kept her place so clean. Every month when she received her welfare check she would buy plenty of food. I loved how she would season and wash the meat before she put it in the refrigerator. She loved to buy her beer to drink. I came to visit one day to share my new place. She was really excited for me. We did not see each other for a while.

One day she showed up at my place, because she did not have a place to stay. Me always remembering being homeless could not turn her away. I told her she could live with me. Everything went well for a while. I would have friends over time to time and started to meet some new friends. I had liked two friends that knew each other. Big mistake one of them came to my house with a friend. He cursed me out and smacked me real hard. I did not want to hear or see him again. I made sure for the future know who you are messing with, but because you don't always know.

Doris's boyfriend came out of jail and "she asked me if he could move in?" I spoke to the landlord who agreed and told them they could have the back room and pay rent. Things went well for a while. After a time, I began to see different people come in & out, all types of drug addicts. They would show up all times during the night and early morning. The landlord was not happy with this activity and I was not either. A friend of mine told me his uncle was a police officer and the place was under surveillance. He told me that they plan on raiding the place and I could lose my children. I did not know what to do helping other people and now I and my children would pay for it.

One day my son could not find his bottle under the bed. I did not have a flash light and used a match. Well the whole place caught on fire and the fire spread through the house. All I could do was grab my two children and leave with the only clothes I had on. I lost all my clothes, my children's clothes and all my food. This was a disaster, but it was like a blessing in disguise, because now I did not have to worry about going to jail. This way Doris and her boyfriend would have to find their own place. I knew the landlord could collect the home insurance and start a new life. The only problem was I had to find a place to stay for my children in the cold winter.

CHAPTER TEN

Being Homeless Again With Two Children

I stood watching the fire burn the house because I had to use a match. A lot of people stood around and offered me and my children to stay for a day or two. They told me the Red Cross was coming. I did not want them to try and take my children, so I went to stay at a rooming house with a white older couple. They had one small bed and was kind enough to let me sleep on the floor. I was able to sleep in the bed with my children. I stayed for a while because I felt I was inconveniencing them. They found some warm clothes for us to wear, so I decided to leave.

I went to visit a lady who lived nearby. She was completing her Thanksgiving dinner. She had the table all set for company. She would not offer me and my children any food. We were so cold and hungry but I had so much pride I did want to beg her for the food, so I asked her for a few dollars she refused to give it to me. I really begged so I could buy my children and me some food, but she would not change her mind. I ran into her years later and she lost her apartment and was living in a room. Her husband left her; he would work two jobs while she fooled around. She must have thought she was going to stay young and beautiful forever, but we all grow old the longer we live oh well. At least years later she saw me in Harlem and told me her story. I told her I was a social worker and was attending the Church Refuge Temple where I had given my life to Christ. She told me I remember you came from nothing to something. We parted ways and I never saw her again I'm sure it was for the best.

As I left her apartment with my two children I wanted to leave them in the warm hallway, because it was so cold outside. I walked down the block to hear them crying, so I went back and we walked out in the cold snow together. This was during November where everyone was celebrating Thanksgiving.

While we were walking the neighborhood junkie of the building saw me. He was the superintendent. He told me I could bring the children to stay with him in the basement. It was not very clean, but warm because the heater was there to warm the building. The place smelled like dried up old blood, because he shot up dope. I can still smell that odor when I think about him. The basement and all his clothes had the same odor, but I needed a place for myself and children to lay our head. We stayed a few days looking for another place to stay, there was a big storm coming.

Eventually I was able to find a kitchenette back in the ghetto area. The place was very small. I started to suffer from severe headaches. The doctor put me on medication. One day when I took the medicine my son turned on the stove to put his shoe on top. I guess he was still having flashbacks about the fire. I called the case worker to tell her I did not want to stay there, she "told me I would have to save the first month's rent and security". They were tired of me changing places and putting up the money. Well I saved the money and was able to get a really nice apartment 1950 Andrews Ave. I stayed there a long time.

CHAPTER ELEVEN

Moving to 1950 Andrews Ave. in the Bronx

I was able to move into my new apartment near New York University College. It was located in the Bronx during the seventies. This was before their new location on West Forth Street located in Manhattan. The surrounding buildings were used to let the college students rent the apartments. The buildings were very huge. They looked like a castle in medieval time. They were located on acres of grass and beautiful trees. The building I moved in had a beautiful garden around all the buildings in a circle. I could look out my window and see the beautiful view. The changes in the seasons were a site to see. I loved the spring season to see the beautiful flowers growing on the trees. My neighbors and I could take the children to the park on the campus grounds. They could ran around and have fun. We would have a picnic and take lots of pictures. I would bring a blanket and food for everyone to eat. Near the building were a daycare, church, and school. I joined the church with the family and enrolled them in school and then after school program at the daycare. The daycare would pick the boy up after school and keep them till 6:00 pm. The pastor of the Catholic Church was very supportive with the families in the community. He would listen to your problems and give you advice. The boys loved going to the church. We all attended the services every Sunday and received Holy Communion. I can remember this day, so well. Calvin and Stanley were praying with their hands together. I had bought them some new outfits and shoes, boy did they look sharp. The church office gave us our Communion papers which I treasure to this day. I also took pictures of this event to save in a picture album. The apartment was huge with large rooms. The boys shared a room with twin beds. I loved to decorate. There was a long foyer with a bar set up. The kitchen was huge connected to the dining area. I was able to have my own washer and dryer. I loved this, since I did like to wash clothes outside. I even bought a large freezer to keep lots of food for the boys. I loved them so much the moon and stars shinned on them. I really spoiled them. We would go bike riding with the neighbor's children. They had lots of friends to play with. I even began to meet people who were attending college. One day I said to myself I was going to go to NYU. I was being surrounded around people who were doing positive things in their lives and it made me want the same for myself and children. I wanted one day to own my own home, travel, and drive a car.

Things were really going great until the devil Ms. Doris showed up with no place to stay. You know I could not turn her away even though she could have had my children taken away and caused me to go to jail. I didn't know I was being setup again. It was hard being homeless myself and strangers allowed me to stay with them. They even slept on the floor. Doris had a few clothes she bought with her. She did well for a while cooking and keeping the place clean. One day she disappeared and never came to get her belonging.

A group of gangsters showed up at my door looking for her. They told me she had left the money with me to pay for drugs. I never messed with drugs in my life, how could she lie, boy did I want to choke her. They told me they would take me on the roof to prostitute unless I came up with the money. I told them I was only getting a small check, but would try to give them what I could every two weeks. They returned like clockwork. They were very tall and scary and would have no problem taking you out this world, and would not look back.

I told my neighbor and she told me her brother was receiving a small monthly check and he would give it to me to pay the drug dealers. I was thankful and mad at the same time to pay for something I didn't owe. I went to look for Doris. She was hiding in another apartment. I could see her through the hole taking drugs. She refused to open the door boy I wish I could have gotten to her for one minute. I walked away and threw her clothes in the garbage and never saw or heard from her again. I continued to pay the men off. They would pick me up and go with me to cash the check. At least I was able to buy food with the check I cashed.

I decided to look for work to pay them off. One day at the welfare office I met this nice looking lady who befriended me. I told her I was looking for work, and she told me her uncle was hiring and could pick me up the following day. He arrived the next day to pick me up. He showed up in an Eldorado car which most pimps would drive. I ignored this hoping for the best. We drove to Manhattan, NY. We went up in a very high building on the twentieth floor. I kept asking "what kind of work do you have"? He didn't answer right away. Once in the apartment which looked like a room in a hotel. The couch bed was open up. I saw a picture of the lady on the table. "I asked him who was she"? "He stated she was a relative and would get girls for him to work with. Now I understand why she would get all fancied up to come to the welfare office where people did not have money to eat or buy decent clothes to wear. She lived in a nice Corp apt with furs and fancy jewelry. The same went for her two attractive girls. They had so much food and new cars. She would bring young women to her place to show off what they could have. It was all a set up."

I never was impressed with other people belonging unless it was mine. At the apartment the pimp told me to look out the window to see his hoes. He told me two would work together. They would bring the client up to the apartment. While one female was in the bed there was another female under the bed to rob him. This could be a very dangerous situation for them. They could even be caught by the client and killed. I wanted to leave his place. "I told him I felt very nervous cause I had left my children with a babysitter and my son had not moved his bowel for days". "He said do you know what a Laxative is"? "I said what that is"? I really knew, but decided to play dumb. He told me some of his hoes get afraid, but there were pills in the bathroom cabinet. He locked the door and told me he would come back. I called my social worker Dorthy Harris who told me to continue to play dumb. When he returned he told me he would take me to the drug store to buy medicine for my baby. He put me in a cab and paid my fare to go home. He gave me his business card which I threw out the window. There was no reason for me to look back. When I arrived home I fell on my knees and thanked God I was not weak or desperate to sell my body for money and clothes. Eventually the pimp and his friend were all caught and sent to jail. What goes around comes around. I eventually paid off the drug dealers their money. With the last check I was able to get my first princess phone, not a cell phone as we use today ha ha my how technology has come, so far. At the end everyone show who they really are. Whatever ends that could be through friendship, good times and bad times.

How can I be loved when I never was loved? How can I appreciate a friend when I never learned to be a friend. How can I trust when my trust was taken away. Some people grow up being disappointed tend to disappoint others that come into their life which destroy good relationship. When you teach someone to think, to be able to make good choices you teach them to survive a long healthy life-style.

CHAPTER TWELVE

**Moving On In Becoming A Mature Young Women,
Still Helping Others**

I continued to open my home to any one that needed food to eat or a place to lay their head. I would have lots of drinks at the red and black bar with lots of mirros behind. My sisters Sarah Majorie, Betty Sonny and my mother would come over. I always cooked I would make some good soul food cooking eg., potato salad, lima beans and hamocks my favourite, collard greens macoroni and cheese fried chicken the works. My boys never had to eat out they always had three home cooked meals. For breakfast I would make pancakes, oat meal and cream farina. I loved to make fruit smoothies from scratch. I always made the boys lunch to take to school. To this day my son never eat out. His older girl friend is a great cook. People would come in and out sometimes spilling drinks and stealing some of my belonging. I decided it was best to cut down on so much entertaining. To many things were coming up missing even television. Sometime we can not help everyone, because everyone don't always appreciate the service. They can feel someone owe them something they did not work for.

They just take things for granted. A lot of times people can look at where you are at but don't know where you came from.

    I decided to let my boy friend Ron move in. He had started to attend college at NYU, he was really smart. He was a good father and good provider. He would work two jobs and bring the money home. He loved my home cooked meals. He gave me the most respect. I was treated like a princess nothing was too good for me and the children. He made sure money was set aside for holidays and school clothes. We had great holidays together. I finally had the perfect family I always dreamed of. No one else matter just my man and my children. It was during, the seventies there was some great songs out. The Temptations, Marvin Gay, the Spinners. We loved to cuddle and listen to the songs. I would even act like I could sing only pretending but it was all good.

    Ron encouraged me to go back to school to get my GED. He said if anything happen to as he wanted to make sure I would have an education. He said he would watch the kids in the evening, so I could go. I went on to receive my GED. Then I went to Malcolm King College to obtain my Associate Degree in Sociology and Psychology. When I start the program they assigned me a counselor and who did you think it was Dorothy Harris. I was so happy to see her. She had changed career from belts a social worker to a college counselor. We caught up on good times. She made sure I took on the right courses, because I was going to become a social worker and eventually retired as a school counselor wow! I had a great future ahead of me. I worked very hard in completing my courses, by making good grades. I finished the program in two years. When I finished Dorothy Harris share with me she was having her first baby and was leaving to go back to her home town. I told her I wanted to attend NYU and she wrote me a beautiful reference which I still have to this day. Everyone said it was very hard to get accepted in NYU, but I was not going to give up. I applied to the school and had to attend a conference with other peers who had come from families that were doctors and lawyers. At the interview I shared my background and they accepted me. I was so excited. I was able to attend the new site in West Fourth Street. It was very nice. The different school building e.g., laws, medicine, social work and many other buildings. There were lots of places to eat healthy food. They also had a large library. There was a church on the grounds of a huge park. I would go there and say a prayer to complete the social work program. I also spent a lot of time getting tutoring. I knew I had not been exposed to some of the life styles as my peers, so I did not feel ashamed if I needed help. I received a two year scholarship and money to purchase school supplies. I worked very hard to complete the program in two years. I graduated with a four year degree from NYU in social work. Dorothy Harris gave me a beautiful graduation card and we said good bye. I wish I could tell her how she helped me and thank her. This is a poem I dedicate to her for being.

The card my counselor gave me when I graduated in June 1980 from NYU reads.

Congratulations!
The studying is over
The exam are done at last
And all those sleepless hours you spent
Are now part of the past
So now its time to have some fun
And really celebrate
Cause how often in a life-time
Can you graduate!!
I am so happy for you!
Always Dorthy Harrise

I thank you for all you did to get me where I am from Barbara Brown a great counselor.

A Counselor's Love
This love will prepare you
For every social situation you will face
It will allow you to cope with life's emotional roller coaster
Because life's ups and downs
Will always be a great challenge
But the love from your counselor
Will guide you into each challenge sucessfully
Only if you're known
The love of your counselor's dream for your life.

Dedicated from Barbara Brown licensed school counselor, to all those school counselor's who gave guidance and love to our children by preparing them to learn positive social skills by becoming life long learners.

Peace & love,
Barabara Brown

CHAPTER THIRTEEN

Moving up in the Bronx 2899 Kings bridge Terrace

After college we decided to move further uptown in the Bronx. Once NYU moved the neighborhood began to change. I was able to find a nice two bedroom near Lehman college. The area was really nice. There were much smaller buildings, but it was very clean. I did miss my old friends, but sometime we have to move on. The boys were still able to have their own room there was a school, church, and after school center. You could walk around the reservoir by the college, it was about two miles. There was a small park near by, and lots of stores on Broadway to go shopping. Transportation was close by. It was a mixed middle class neighborhood. The children were doing well in school. I started a job working with teenagers in the foster care system as a case worker. There was a church near by, so we joined as a family. We would even have bible study at different people's house. Everyone would bring food to share. One of the young men asked me "did I even think about becoming a teacher"? "I told him now" "he said you could have the hours as the children and the same holidays". Ron and I had gotten married and he wanted us to go in to the army.

I told him I would wait till he return, because I wanted to get my Masters in Education. I really wanted a stable life for the boys and was happy where we were living. He made the decision to go which was a mistake. He developed a rare disease which caused his death later on and became disabled. This was very hard for me he always wrote us, but it was not the same.

I signed up at Lehman college to obtain my first Masters in Education. I bought an used car to get around. I would sheak out to practice and almost hit some people's car. They yelled at me in the window ???. I did learn to drive and would go all over with Nelly Bell. One day while driving a hole was in the bottom of the floor I could see the street moving. Nelly Bell was a small orange buggy, but she sure got around. Everyone knew when I came home late from church. The car would make these loud banging noises. A mechanic placed a metal plate over the hole. Me and the boys would drive upstate to bear mountains. They really enjoyed that. They were teenagers and had made friends of their own. They were really good boys. Stanley was spoiled, he loved to play basketball. Calvin loved to work and save his money. To this day he still hold on to every penny.

I completed my masters in two years. It was difficult to write a thesis, but I did it. I started working in a daycare center part time and had got some experience. I got a job with the Board of Education with a first grade class. I was able to be home with the boys, but I still wanted to do social work or counseling. The Social Work Masters program wanted you to do a two days full time internship. I had a family and needed to make a living. I met my friend Emma RIP we became very good friends, since we were both teachers. I also began to make friends with other professionals who were working hard. I worked at the school for one year.

Ron had put in for a new upcoming high riser in Starett City in Brooklyn NY. They had informed me that they had a two bedroom available for me and the boys, so I started packing and moved. The building was seventeen floors high. Our apartment was located on the thirteenth floor. Everything was new, the floor were ??? and the cabinets were white wood. The school was on the premises. We had a view overlooking the lake and the Verrazano Bridge. There was acers of grass and trees with large basketballs courts. They also had a large health club and boxing club. The boys could go to the teen program after school. I felt like the song by "The Jefferson's moving on up". I got a job as a teacher nearby and was able to buy a Toyota new car. It was colored a light gold. I could drive back and forth from work and pick the boys up. All the teachers at work had their own cars. I also joined church with the boys close by. We would go every Sunday and Wednesday for prayer. There also was a shopping center in walking distance. I also had a parking spot in a indoor garage.

    I met a few new teachers and starting take vacations. A few of the teachers would travel together. We visit different countries, and took cruises. The boys had become young men and started to date. I made sure they always had protection not to have unwanted children. I started to date, but it did work out because the men did not want a commitment. I was in my thirties and still wanted companionship since Ron was in the army, and we had been separated a few years. The only problem was some men looked for women to be a sugar momma. They wanted to move in and you cook for them. I decided it wasn't for me, so I started Ministry school. I always worked two jobs and attended school at night. I kept very busy. It can keep you out of trouble.

CHAPTER FOURTEEN

The Death of Stanley Brown by a Bully

We all had settled in the new place. Stanley RIP loved to play basketball outside with his friend till the night. I could always hear his laughter. He was always smiling and telling me jokes. I was very close to him because he was my baby son. I would buy him anything he wanted. He loved to wear the latest shoes and clothes. He loved my cooking and would eat up all of the leftover. He was loved by everyone in the community even the adults loved him. He would never drink or smoke. When he was twelve a pastor prophesied to him that he would not do either.

One day he complained of a boy bothering him every time he saw him. I told him to avoid the boy. He was seeing a young lady and they fell in love. He talked to me about getting married but I told both of them were not ready. He was only eighteen and lived a sheltered life. He and his brother really never had to work hard except to have spending money. He loved to eat, sleep and watch TV with his friends. He had plenty of friends everyone from all races they loved him. They loved to hang in his bedroom lying on the floor and the bed. They both did not listen. One day I came home from work and they had packed up and went to New Jersey. When I looked in the draw and saw his clothes gone, this really hurt me. The young lady had convinced him to leave, so they could get married.

After a few days things did not go so well he called me up to come get him. By now Ron had come out the army, but wanted to live alone because he was sick. He did not want to be a burden on me. He wanted to be close to his family. We drove and bought Stanley back to Brooklyn. I was beginning to have these strange dreams over and over again. I just could not shake them I even asked for prayer, but they would not go away. It was like I was falling or dreaming of object falling. One evening I was waiting for my neighbor to pick me up to go exercise, but she didn't show or call. I lay down to take a nap, when I heard a bang at the door. "My neighbor yelled Stanley has been stabbed. I opened the door to see blood all over his yellow plastic hooded jacked he wanted me to buy. I told him to lay down, so I could call the police. For some reason the phone wouldn't work. A voice came to me to tell my son to ask for forgiveness. I put the phone down to tell him to talk to God it was nothing I could do. He started to pray and "I told him he was going to be alright". At first "he had said it was dark" and collapsed, but when he came back "he said I am back". He continues to talk and pray very quietly. I ran back to call 911. When I heard him say "good by mom I'm going" "I told him he could not go" but he just hit the floor hard. By then his friends and the ambulance had arrived and began to work on him, but to me he was gone. I could feel the presence of angels in the whole house I just began to praise God. It was a feeling I never experience. I felt like when you are in church and the people are praising God.

I went in the ambulance to the hospital but the doctor said he had done all he could. I went home to clean up all the blood on the floor and elevator. Then I just started to scream. I took all his clothes and threw them down the chute for the garbage. I took care of all the service for the funeral alone. A lot of people came from all over to visit they would cook and clean, but I just felt numb. I stopped eating and did not go to work. I was really depressed until one of the teachers told me to fix myself up. The funeral was held in a large church. The principal of my school allowed any one who wanted to attend the service could leave work.

The loss of a child is the worst thing a parent would never want to go through. People say time heals wounds, but "I say only time passes but you will always remember their smile, laughter, their birthday, the day of their death, holidays and mother's day is the worst." You don't like people to remind you only when you want to talk. I feel like they should not bring it up unless I want to. It has to be my own private conversation not their's.

The boy that had commited the crime was out on bail. He was the one that had bullied my son. He had saw him at a party and started a fight with my son's friend. My son took up for his friend and and the bully got into a fight. My son won the fight and the boy threaten his life. Anytime someone threaten you it should be taken very seriously. I had told the police when my son told me, but they just took it as words, by "saying nothing happened."

Something did happen and the bully kept his word. While he was out on bail he walked around the complex joking and laughing. When I came from work he would be outside with his friends. One day I started to carry a knife and would watch him in my car. Then my other son had a knife under his pillow, so I took both our knives and through them away. It was not worth me going to jail or my son. I was not going to lose another child. The bully stayed out for a while then he was put in jail for fifteen years. He wrote me a letter to tell me he was sorry, but I have to forgive him, so I can move on, being angry is not going to bring my Stanley back. I will be buried next to him at Pine Lawn Cemetery when my time comes. I know I will see him in heaven with the angels, so I live right each day of my life until God call me home to be his servant in his glorious kingdom. Where there will be no more death, sickness, or shedding of tears. He's going to wipe all that away, now that I'm sixty three we are closer than we think. The main this is to always love and have a forgiving heart. I always remember that song ??? to men of how we all miss our love ones, so I dedicated this poem to my son Stanley Brown RIP.

The love of Someone We Lost
I know I have lost someone but now I have to move on
I know realize they have touched my life and how
I must touch others
Life is like a circle and we must keep
Moving on, but the love we shared will never stop
Dedicated to my beloved son Stanley Brown who was
lost to violence and showed me the true meaning of love of
of a son for 18 years and was a great friend and brother to Calvin Brown.

RIP Love Mom

CHAPTER FIFTEEN

Moving on Forward to Except and Forgive, But Not Forget

I called the management office in the complex to ask if I could move. The memories always remind me of that cold day February 16,1990 which I will remember as it was yesterday. They said "There was a vacant apartment in another building," so my son and I packed up to move. The apartment had been renovated and was in great shape. The only thing was it was located on the thirteen floor the same where I moved from. It still was a change not to be so close to the other place. Sometime when I have to go pass I get a knot in my stomach I dreamt about my son a few times. In each dream he was moving farther away till he never came to me again.

I continue to stay busy with my job working with the children. I continued in ministry school and completed the five year program. One year I was chosen salutatorian June 1993. I graduate from the school.

A little while later my husband Ron passed away. I will always remember him for the love he gave us. I know he is still looking down on me. I never found a man who showed me, so much love. I miss him being around to talk to. He would give me the most beautiful cards. He had a elegant handwriting I saved all his cards he gave me. Here are some of the words from his cards.

Barbara Brown

For My Wife 2/14/87
*Once in a life time
You find someone special
Your lives in ??? And
Somehow you know This is
the beginning of all you have
longed for. A love you can
build on A love that will grow
Once in a lifetime To those who
are lucky A miracle happens
And dreams all come true I
Know it can happen, It happen
to me. For I've found My
Once in a life time with you
With all my love on Valentine's Day
And Always I Love You Barbara
Ambassador Cards.*

Shattered Not Broken by Living Victoriously Through the Holy Spirit

I dedicate this poem to you Ronnie RIP

You Are Never Alone
*The love you had
Will encourage you
Through difficult times
When you feel alone.
You are never alone
When you have cried all
You can you will remember
the love you had and your
mind will become clear
And you will smile at the
great sunshine that
will appear. Then you will
never feel alone again
Because now you see the
real meaning of those who
Share true spiritual love
God's Love.*

Love from your wife forever,
Barbara Brown

CHAPTER SIXTEEN

Returning Back to College

I always wanted to do counseling with families and children. Working in the school as a teacher, children were becoming more challenging. Many children's parents had turn to the drug crack and had to be place in the foster care system. Some of them would move in with other relatives. There were a lot of children who were living in single housholds mostly with the mother. There were few fathers in the home. This was very difficult for boys who did not have positive role models in their home. Most of them lived with different family female the aunt, mother, and grandmother's control the household. The fathers were dating different women in the same community having children and moving on to the next one. Children were becoming very angry with this new lifestlye. They were getting into a lot of fights and the parents were just as angry. They would come to the school and want to yell and scream at the staff. Most of them were collecting welfare and food stamp. They would have different children with different men. Some of the men were involved and the others were not. The children would become angry when they did not get to see their dads. Sometimes the mothers would keep the children from them as a punishment. This was being filtered in the class and began to make my job as a teacher more difficult.

I decided by going to college I could use more training in dealing with their social issues. A lot of the students needed counseling, but the parents did not want to get them the help they needed. As a counselor I would be better prepare to give the students more support, so they could focus on their classwork, instead of being stressed out with problems from home.

I registered for the counseling program at Brooklyn College. I also completed the Advanced Certificate Program. I worked very hard in school. I received a second master and advanced degree in guidnace and counseling. I took the test and was given a license to counsel families and children in school. I left my job as a teacher for sixteen years in East Brooklyn, NY and became a school counselor in Bedsty.

I was really proud of myself I had my office and was glad to be out the classroom. I decorated my office, so nicely with pictures of children coping with social skills. I really enjoyed my work. I would set up groups with the student to discuss different issues they were dealing with. They also could play games like checkers and chess. They also love to put puzzles together. There were writing workshop on how to control their anger.

During the winter I started a coat drive for children who did not have coats for the winter. I love to see their happy face when they had a warm coat during the cold months. I always kept belts for the boys who let their pants hang down. These belt were too small for me and my waist will never set that small. I also would keep hair combs for children who parents were too lazy to do their hair. I found free eye glass clinics who were willing to give the children free eye glasses and exams. I would go with groups of children to take them. After their exam we would go to a fast food place of their choice. They mostly liked Mcdonald.

During lunch time I would sit with the children and listen to their stories. Students of today are very out spoken. It's different when I was growing up. They love to say whats on their mind they made me laugh. They loved that I was happy all the time. At home it was very different they would say their moms never smile. We would jump rope after lunch they love to jump rope with me.

Time was passing and I began to start feeling tired. I was written up in the daily newspaper for starting the mentoring program. I also received two community award from the neighborhood community program that reached out the families. They were very helpful with children in foster homes. They allowed me to choose children that did good writing. If their writing was selected they were able to have their writings in the agencies magazine. I enjoyed the years I worked with children, but I was approaching thirty years of service and was ready to retire to Florida. I had published four books and plan on writing more. I want to thank all the children I had the pleasure of meeting. I pray they will do great things. I hope I live long enough to be proud of them as their school counselor. The same way my counselor would be proud of me.

Shattered Not Broken by Living Victoriously Through the Holy Spirit

I dedicate this poem to all my student I had contact with.

Love for Our Children

Children from the day you were born
people and animals will come into your lives
It may be your parents, uncles, aunts, grandparents,
foster parents, you never know who?
Each of their purpose is to show us love
They could also be all school staff, teachers,
principals, counselors, para custodian
There can be no limit
But the love we are given from each
allows us to fullfill all our dreams
as we grow into adult we will remember
the role they played in our lives and thank them always.
But you will never know the true
meaning of love until you have experienced it!

Dedicated to all the children of the world

Love & Peace,
Barbara Brown

CHAPTER SEVENTEEN

Retiring and Moving to Florida

I put in all my paper work to retire June 2013. I started pack up all my belonging to take home. It was a funny feeling to be leaving the school. I really grew up there from my thirty's to my early sixty's. As I packed I kept looking around and though, about how time just flies it seem like the other day I was a young women with a barbie doll shape and now I have a middle age shape. I came in with a head full of hair, but now it has got thinner and some gray, but least I have my health and glad. I could retire and do what ever I want to. I do not have to listen to any boss. Now I am my own boss. I can get up when I want to and go to bed when I want to, there is no more schedule. The phone rang and one of the staff members said the principal want to see you at the graduation. I was really surprised. I went to the church, because it was graduation day. I took a seat in the back. The principal called me up to the front to present me with flowers and a ??? which quoted "A state of mind Living Victoriously not bind by circumsance."

It is so funny the word victoriously is part of the title of my book. I walked back to my office for the last time. I finished packing the last of my beloging and walked out the door I looked around saying to myself like "Jesus said on the cross it is finished. I was a little sad to be leaving sad and happy feeling. I really don't like goodbye's. So I walked out the back door, for the last time.

    I had purchased a Condo in Florida in a retired community. It is really nice and quiet. There are no children around they just come to visit. There is a large golf club with beautiful palm trees. They also have a Tennis court and club house for people to go for entertainement. There is transportion to escort you back and forth if you don't drive. My dog and birds love it out here Domino love to go for his daily walk or he will make you miserable if you don't take him out. He is my best friend I tell people Jesus first, me, and my animals. I love to dress him up and tell him how cute he is. I even dedicated a poem to my animals. I had a cat for eighteen years named Pierre I really miss him. Before he passed away he waited till I woke up to say goodbye. I had him cremated and his ashes spread near my son.

    I wrote this poem for animals.

Love from you pet

Let's not forget those time when you felt alone.
And our pet's always came to comfort us not expecting anything in return
Always having so much compassion
Their look of love shows how much they care
And let us know they will be there each time we need them
So never forget your pet whose love them will never leave
But will be there through those precious moments with a great big smile!

Dedicated to my beloved cat Pierre who gave me 18 years of happiness. I will forever miss you. Thank you Domino, sassy and spicy for being with me.

Love Forvever,
Barbara Brown

I love my condo it is nice and cozy with a lot of space. I get to see the sunset and rise over the beautiful lakes. People are really nice when you go to the stores. Most of them try to treat you very nice. I really love the weather during the winter. I wrote a poem called

Winter in the summer in Florida
Tall palm trees swaying in the wind
Green grass with the smell of summer
Lady bug crawling on the walls
Sunshine all day
Butterfly flying around
Lizards running around
Ducks swimming on the lake
With their babies cross the road
freely. Senior golfing all day
and riding their bikes
People wearing shorts and sandles
With the feel of the warm air
Against their skin. No matter how
Your day began you can always
feel good from the winter in Florida
during the day and end with the
night with the windows wide open
As you settle in for the night

Peace,
Barbara Brown

I dedicate this poem to myself and all those people who get to retire

Retirement
Receive what God has for your life
Enjoy rest and do nothing for all your fruits of your labor
Trust in God to see you through everything
You have to surrender all.
Interesting things will come to you from God
you couldn't imagine
Receive what God wants for your life
Enjoy all the things God gives to sustain us
through the good and bad times
Means to a new chapter of our lives.

Entertain yourself with all the things you were not able to do and say. Now you don't need other's approval as you did in the past you only need God's. Sometimes he allows as to go through the lowest point in our lives so we can lean on and trust him.

Never give up because we have to know God has brought us through this far and he will never leave us or forsake us.

I hope reading about the tribulations and challenges I faced will give you the support you need to complete your retirement. Some of us are in denial. We only live for the moment. We are not concerned about what goes on around us. We continue to live from moment to moment. We are not concerned for the furutre. We are only satisfied today. We are blessed to be the best. Be thankful for those who are there for you and forgive those who are not. Let go and Let God reveal what he has for the next chapter in your life. Learn to trust and depend on God not in some people who take advantage during your weakness. They watch and wait for you to fall. Why are we here? Life is living to support others and ourselves. Our lives don't belong to us only to God do we belong. Dont worry about people from your past.

There is a reason they did not make it into your future. Be transformed by the renewing of your mind. Stop letting people talk you out of what God has called you to be and have. When you ask the approval of your critics you give them the power. We have a right to be happy. Be arrounded people who add positive things to your life or God will have someone do it for you. People should not be estimated by your success. You should be acepted not tortured by the wrong people. God does not give us the power of fear, but of a sound mind. At the end everyone shows who they really are, whatever end that could be good or bad.

God Bless

Peace & Love
Barbara Brown

www.ingramcontent.com/pod-product-compliance
Lightning Source LLC
Chambersburg PA
CBHW032214040426
42449CB00005B/583